READING POWER

Westward Ho!

THE U.S. CAVALRY AND THE INDIAN WARS

EMILY RAABE

The Rosen Publishing Group's
PowerKids Press™
New York

Published in 2003 by The Rosen Publishing Group, Inc.
29 East 21st Street, New York, NY 10010

First Edition

Book Design: Michael DeLisio

Photo Credits: Cover (top) Northwestern University Library, Edward S. Curtis's "The North American Indian," the Photographic Images; cover (bottom), pp. 20–21 © Library of Congress, Prints and Photographs Division; pp. 4–5, 6–7, 8–9, 11 (top) © Hulton/Archive/Getty Images; p. 10 Michael DeLisio; pp. 11 (bottom), 12, 13, 14–15, 17, 18–19 © North Wind Picture Archives; pp.16, 19 (inset), 21 (inset) © Denver Public Library, Western History Collection, images X-31891, NS-102, X-31254

Library of Congress Cataloging-in-Publication Data

Raabe, Emily.
The U.S. Cavalry and the Indian Wars / Emily Raabe.
  p. cm. — (Westward ho!)
Summary: Describes the conflicts between Native Americans and European settlers as settlements were established farther and farther west.
Includes bibliographical references (p.) and index.
ISBN 0-8239-6496-5 (lib. bdg.)
1. Indians of North America—Wars—Juvenile literature. [1. Indians of North America—Wars.] I. Title.
E81 .R33 2003
973—dc21

2002001800

JNF
973
Raabe

Contents

The First Settlers

The first English settlement in America was at Jamestown, Virginia, in 1607. In the beginning, the settlers got along well with the Native Americans who lived in the area. However, in 1622, the Native Americans and the settlers began to fight.

Jamestown burned down three times. People finally left Jamestown in 1699 to move inland.

Jamestown was named after King James I of England.

5

In the 1700s and 1800s, more European settlers came to America. Fighting between settlers and Native Americans went on all over the country. There were battles in New England, the Southwest, the South, and the Midwest. All of this fighting would later be called the "Indian Wars."

Some Native Americans helped the early settlers farm. Sometimes, the settlers bought land from the Native Americans.

Different Ways of Living

The settlers and Native Americans lived differently and didn't understand one another. This made them dislike and fear each other.

Native Americans hunted and fished for food and clothing. The settlers cut down forests in order to make fields and grow food. This took away the hunting grounds from the Native Americans.

Native Americans needed buffalo for food and clothing. In the western United States, settlers killed buffalo and sold the skins.

Settlers continued to move to the rich lands east of the Mississippi River. It was soon clear that the settlers and Native Americans could not live in peace near each other. The settlers wanted the Native Americans to leave. The U.S. government ordered the Native Americans to move west.

Native Americans forced into the West

Mississippi River

Settlers moving westward

In 1830, the U.S. government passed the Indian Removal Act. This law forced Native Americans to move west of the Mississippi River.

Settlers often traveled together in groups called wagon trains. They helped each other along the way and camped together at night.

In 1848, gold was found in California. Suddenly, thousands of settlers wanted to travel west of the Mississippi River to look for gold. As they passed through the lands that the Native Americans lived on, some of the settlers decided they wanted to live there, too. However, they did not want to live with the Native Americans.

The U.S. government bought land from Native Americans so that settlers could farm or look for gold.

Settlers traveling west often passed through land that still belonged to Native Americans.

RESERVATION LIFE

Native Americans were sent to live on reservations. They did not like living on these lands. They could not move around or hunt freely.

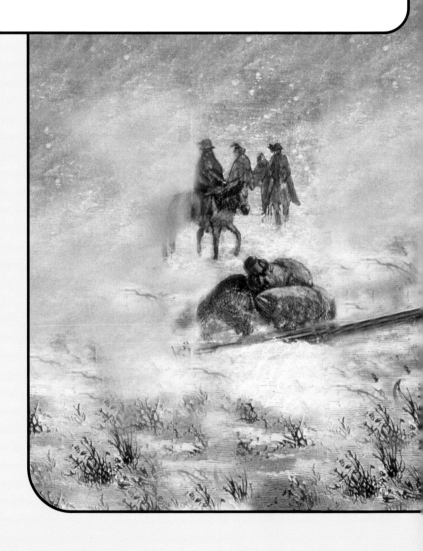

Most Native Americans were angry that their land had been taken from them. More fighting between Native Americans and settlers began.

Native Americans often had trouble finding enough food to eat on the reservations. These lands were not very good for farming.

The government sent the cavalry of the U.S. Army to fight the Native Americans. The Sioux (*SOO*) Wars lasted from 1854 to 1890. The most famous battle was on June 25, 1876. The U.S. Cavalry, led by George Armstrong Custer, attacked a group of Sioux near Little Bighorn, Montana.

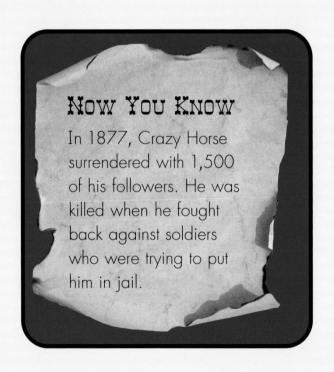

Now You Know

In 1877, Crazy Horse surrendered with 1,500 of his followers. He was killed when he fought back against soldiers who were trying to put him in jail.

Crazy Horse and his Sioux warriors killed Custer (standing, with rifle) and about 210 U.S. soldiers during the Battle of Little Bighorn.

THE END OF THE INDIAN WARS

On December 4, 1890, Sioux chief Sitting Bull was killed when he refused to be arrested by the cavalry. A battle followed near Wounded Knee Creek in South Dakota.

In the fighting, 180 Native Americans and 25 cavalry soldiers were killed. It was the last big battle of the Indian Wars, ending over 250 years of fighting.

Sitting Bull

Battles between Native Americans and the U.S. Cavalry were fought at a close distance and often ended very quickly.

The settlers and Native Americans could not find a way to live together. The Native Americans lost almost all of their land by the time the Indian Wars ended.

After 1869, railroads allowed people to travel quickly across the country. Many people moved to the West.

The settlers had moved into every part of America to make a better life for themselves. The Indian Wars changed America forever.

When European settlers first came to America, there were about one million Native Americans living there. By the end of the Indian Wars, only about 237,000 Native Americans remained.

Glossary

arrested (uh-**rehst**-uhd) having been put in jail for breaking the law

buffalo (**buhf**-uh-loh) a large animal related to the cow

cavalry (**kav**-uhl-ree) soldiers who were trained to fight on horseback

Native Americans (**nay**-tihv uh-**mehr**-uh-kuhnz) the first people to live on the lands that became America

reservations (rehz-uhr-**vay**-shuhnz) lands that were set aside for Native Americans by the U.S. government

settlement (**seht**-l-muhnt) a place where people come to live

settlers (**seht**-luhrz) people who come to stay in a new country or place

surrendered (suh-**rehn**-duhrd) to have given up

warriors (**wor**-ee-uhrz) people who fight in wars

Resources

Books

Crazy Horse's Vision
by Joseph Bruchac
Lee and Low Books (2000)

Sitting Bull: Lakota Leader
by Catherine Iannone
Franklin Watts (1999)

Web Sites

Due to the changing nature of Internet links, PowerKids Press has developed an on-line list of Web sites related to the subjects of this book. This site is updated regularly. Please use this link to access the list:

http://www.powerkidslinks.com/wh/usca/

Index

Word Count: 475

Note to Librarians, Teachers, and Parents

If reading is a challenge, Reading Power is a solution! Reading Power is perfect for readers who want high-interest subject matter at an accessible reading level. These fact-filled, photo-illustrated books are designed for readers who want straightforward vocabulary, engaging topics, and a manageable reading experience. With clear picture/text correspondence, leveled Reading Power books put the reader in charge. Now readers have the power to get the information they want and the skills they need in a user-friendly format.